For Jane Ho

I hope my story bring
understanding to you about connecting
God while traveling + knowing that there's
nothing wrong praying to Miss God
who gives us the ability to
travel because so many people
wish they could travel but
circumstances want let them
travel. Be Blessed

This book will touch many traveling people that don't know
how to contact God by traveling on the highway.

THE LIFE
OF A PRAYING
OWNER-OPERATOR

My Destination Is Heaven
Volume I

J. D. MILAM

WESTBOW
PRESS®
A DIVISION OF THOMAS NELSON
& ZONDERVAN

Scripture taken from the King James Version of the Bible.

WestBow Press books may be ordered through booksellers or by contacting:

WestBow Press
A Division of Thomas Nelson & Zondervan
1663 Liberty Drive
Bloomington, IN 47403
www.westbowpress.com
844-714-3454

ISBN: 978-1-5127-9385-7 (sc)
ISBN: 978-1-5127-9386-4 (hc)
ISBN: 978-1-5127-9384-0 (e)

Library of Congress Control Number: 2017910994

Print information available on the last page.

WestBow Press rev. date: 05/18/2021

CONTENTS

Part I.   Patience

Chapter 1:   The Life of Trucking 1

Chapter 2:   Traveling Is a Blessing 9

Chapter 3:   Getting Up Early and Lying Down Late ... 17

Chapter 4:   Praying All Around the Clock.....................27

Chapter 5:   Can't Make It Home for Dinner.................33

Chapter 6:   My Destination Is Coming Up.....................39

Chapter 7:   Honey, I'm Home 43

Part II. Resting

Chapter 8:   No Stress: All the Bills Are Paid 51

Chapter 9:   Never Get Out of Your Truck......................57

Chapter 10:   Treat Every Trip Like A Vacation 63

Chapter 11:   Breaker One Nine....................................69

Chapter 12:   Trucking Is a Career 75

Chapter 13:   Going the Wrong Way................................81

Chapter 14:   My Destination Is Heaven..........................85

Notes 91

Trucker Guide...97

Part I

PATIENCE

INSPIRATION AND ACKNOWLEDGMENTS

Keonya N. Milam, my loving and caring wife, you are the Queen of our Castle, the key to my ignition. My love for you is stronger than unsweetened coffee, and you have given me our daughter—a princess I always dreamed of. Because of your support and your belief in me, I will continue to lead my family. Thank you. I love you.

To my mother, Queen Ada Mae Milam, the world's greatest mom: Thank you for your commitment to all your children. You are the strongest woman I know and a prayer warrior. I love you.

Grandmother Beatrice Milam, known as Big Mama, you are an all-around mother who knows Jesus. Grandmother Minnie P. Mosley, you are the sweetest grandmother I know. And Grandmother Eva Huddleston, you are a softhearted and kind woman of God. You have all shown me true standards of praying and building my faith in the Most High God.

To my dad, Louis J. Mosley, who taught me how to drive: Without this experience I wouldn't be where I am today. Thank you, Dad!

To my Aunt Patricia, Aunt Kay, Aunt Thelma Mosley, Aunt Dorothy, and Aunt Minnie Milam: If it hadn't been for your support over the years, I don't know where I would be today. You are the greatest aunt's in the world. Thank you all.

To my Uncle Kenneth W. Mosley, who introduced me to the Bible, and to the trucking world: You taught me how to drive a stick shift. You told me that I would need this throughout my life, and I know for sure that you were right. Thank you for your commitment and dedication. You are the reason I chose a career in transportation.

Uncle Sherman E. Mosley, thank you for your dedication to the trucking industry. I've watched you over the years travel the highway with no complaints. You know how to take care of business like a trucker should, and because of you I'm faithful. Thank you.

To my father in the ministry Dr. Abraham L. Kennard: You are a true apostle, evangelist, prophet, pastor, teacher, friend, prayer warrior, mentor, and something like a dad. You have taken me under your wing and directed me down the right path, leading me in the Word of God. Thank you.

Thank all of you for the support you have given me as I have pursued my dreams. Thank you for leading me down the right path. And I thank you, Lord, for being the cornerstone of it all.

When I was a kid I always wanted a remote-control truck and trailer, but for several years, the only kind I got was the kind I had to push with my hands. On the day I finally received a real remote-control truck, no one was able to tell me anything. I was a happy little kid. Even then I had a vision of owning my own trucking company.

Trucking has been in my family my whole life. I just love trucking. I know it may sound strange, but I love the smell of diesel. I grew up watching my Uncle Kenny and Uncle Sherman clean their trucks. Every Saturday morning I'd go out in the yard with Uncle Kenny and help him clean his truck. He would let me start it up. I loved the whistling sound I heard every time I pushed the pedal. I really enjoyed the alligator sound I heard when I hit the Jake brake button when we were rolling. It scares people sometimes as traffic approaches a red light. You can see people slowing down or even moving out the way of the truck.

If people understood what truckers really do for the world, they would give truckers better respect. Trucking is my desire. If it wasn't for my Uncle Kenny and Uncle Sherman, I might not have learned that trucking was the career for me. I thank you both and appreciate you for the time you put in with me. Because of the seed you planted in me, my life has never been the same. Thank you for your commitment, and most of all I thank the Lord for allowing you to do what you did around me to motivate me to carry on in my life. Thank you!

I grew up in a place that made me feel like I was in slavery. This county had no streetlights, and there was hardly any traffic ever traveling on the roads. The only things I saw most of the time were trees. I always wondered what my life would be like living in the city. I prayed daily to the Father asking him to change my situation, and it finally happened, but I never forgot the standards or manners with which I was raised. I carried my moral values with me from the country to the city; they are what keeps me humble. It's as if I have had a taste of two worlds, and to me it's an advantage—like speaking two languages.

My purpose in this world is to love and to serve. I'm driven by faith in what the Lord has put in me to move and operate the way he wants me too. My vision is kingdom business, but my driving force is transportation, and I don't see it going anywhere anytime soon. I see the Lord moving more people behind the wheels of tractor-trailers and positioning them to have more of a serving attitude than a taker attitude.

My trucking career was a desire from above, but my experience was inspired by Western Express, a well-known trucking company in the Nashville, Tennessee, area, which gave me the opportunity to sharpen my skills as a driver and later on become an owner-operator. I thank the Lord for directing my path in choosing McNeil Express for the training and Western Express for the experience that I have now in trucking. As of today, I'm still a friend to the company. Thank you all for playing a major part on this journey in my life. Thank you, Western Express. God Bless you and everyone else.

Jason Devon Milam

Charge them that are rich in this world,
that they be not high minded, nor trust in
uncertain riches, but in the living God, who
giveth us richly all things to enjoy; That
they do good, that be rich in good works,
ready to distribute, willing to communicate;
Laying up in store for themselves a good
foundation against the time to come,
that they may lay hold on eternal Life.
(1 Timothy 6:17–19)

Chapter 1

THE LIFE OF TRUCKING

First things first: have you accepted who you are as a human being? Have you found your niche in this world? I think I have found mine. I've been blessed with a desire to do something that the whole world needs. My desire is trucking. The trucking industry has been around for a long time and will be around until the Lord comes back. Trucks are needed everywhere because of the high demand for our basic needs in the world. Think about it for a moment. Can an airplane unload at a Walmart supercenter? Name any location, and you'll see what brings the freight to the customer. Trucks run the world. Trains move most of the world's freight, but it takes a tractor-trailer to get it from a rail yard to a distribution center.

My life changed the first time I sat behind the wheel of an eighteen-wheeler. I was nervous at first. But because I had been around trucking as a kid, the fear disappeared, and I went to a truck-driving school. My dream has now come to pass. I was in school twenty-one days and then spent thirty days on the road with a trainer. I enjoyed being at the school and met some cool people as well. I had a lot in common with one of the guys I met there. We wanted the same things out of life and are still friends today; we think of each other as brothers.

At school, when I finished taking all the tests, the real test came. Four coordinators took everyone to a site where there was concrete padding as far as we could see. Ten trucks and trailers were lined up side by side between orange emergency cones. I was so excited that the time had come. I had learned a bit about driving trucks from my uncles and had to act as if I didn't know anything so the trainers could teach me everything. Sometimes when you know too much of the things teachers are talking about, they seem to pull back on giving you 100 percent of training.

The coordinators chose four people and told each of them to get into a truck; there were forty guys at the school. The coordinators showed us all what to do a couple of times so we could practice daily. After that, we were on our own to help each other. I didn't make it look obvious that I knew what I knew. We had to pull the truck forward a hundred yards and then back it up a hundred yards—over and over until everyone got the routine down. Once everyone got the hang of it, we were off to the races. It was exciting to see guys like me wanting to drive a truck, and after the first day, everyone was amped about trucking.

We did the same things over and over every day until the coordinators saw we had it. Each day they added new routines to our drive to spice up our training. We had to make right turns, left turns, and set the truck in an S position before backing into a dock.

Then the time came to get on the highway. I never had butterflies until we got on the interstate. The problem wasn't me driving; the problem was having to deal with someone else controlling the wheel. This was a nerve-racking experience, but we did it. I passed the road test. The coordinator asked me, "Are you sure this is your first time?" We all just laughed it off. Only one person on the truck knew I could do it, and we are still brothers today.

After passing the road test I was put with a trainer for thirty days. This guy was from the Virgin Islands. He was a different kind of guy. He wanted to drive in the daylight and make me drive after dark. The first couple of nights he stayed up to see if I had it, and after that, he went to bed. My uncle had taught me how to take it easy on the clutch so I wouldn't rock the truck too hard. When the trainer got up every day, he would tell me, "You are driving this truck like you have been driving for years." I felt good about myself when I heard these things from someone with experience. I knew then I would be okay on the truck by myself.

I hardly slept when he was driving. He seemed to forget that I was in the bed, and he would play his music loud while I tried to sleep. He hit every bump and woke me up with every single one of them. I often prayed while going through this: "Lord Jesus, give me the strength to push on." Can you imagine riding with someone you barely know and then falling asleep? Trusting someone else to drive safely while you're resting can be a major risk. We traveled from Little Rock, Arkansas, to Los Angeles, California, and then from Los Angeles to San Antonio, Texas, and back to Little Rock for the entirety of my thirty days. That was a long thirty days.

I was making only $300 a week while I was in training. I felt as if I had been played, used, and not properly compensated after watching this guy go into the mall and come out with so many bags. He felt bad for me and bought me a pair of shoes. I did all the running, and he got all the money for the runs. I couldn't wait to get out of his truck. It was very hard training with this guy, but what he didn't know was that, as I was observing his mistakes, I was becoming wiser and sharpening my skills.

I'll never forget one particular time in Laredo, Texas. We didn't have a load on the weekend, so we stayed at a truck stop the whole time. It was Saturday night, and we were sitting there with our CB (citizens band radio) on. A guy with a Spanish accent came across the air and asked if anybody wanted to go to Mexico to see a drunk donkey, and if we did, we should turn our CB to channel 9. My trainer got excited and turned to channel 9. The guy on the CB called himself "Cadillac Man." He came to the truck stop in a black Cadillac limo. The requirement to go was $30 a person, and he told us we'd get a free cold beer on the way. We crossed the border and paid only fifty cents. We paid nine more US dollars for a taxi to take us from the border to a place called Boise Towne (pronounced like "Boys Town," a village in Nebraska). Everyone there spoke fluent Spanish except for one guy who spoke English and Spanish. He led us to the show, and we bought him something to drink. He was very thankful. They got the donkey drunk, and the donkey fell down over and over again. I was ready to go back, but we had to stick together because we had come together. My trainer was drinking and enjoying himself. I had to be alert because I was in an uncomfortable place.

We finally left there and went to a bar where we thought

there would be girls. It turned out they were all guys dressed like women. Some of them looked just like women; you couldn't see their Adam's apples. I said, "Lord Jesus, save me." The good thing was that I stayed sober just to be on the safe side in case I had to run. We had to stay in a rundown hotel in Boise Towne until morning because of a miscommunication with the taxi driver. I said I would never go back to Boise Towne, and I'd never mentioned it to anyone until now. I laugh at this experience now, since Christ has saved me. This could have turned out badly— crossing the border and not knowing what we were getting ourselves into. The taxi picked us up the next morning and took us back to the border, and we paid fifty cents to reenter the United States.

When we made it back to the truck, we had a run from San Antonio to Los Angeles, and from there back to Little Rock. When we made it back, the trainer reported that I had done a great job, so I was released from him that day.

The company gave me an owner-operator truck. I don't know how I ended up with it, but I was excited. It was a round-nose 2004 Peterbilt 387 with a clean black paint job. I didn't have it long because someone at the company saw me on the interstate in it, and that made him jealous. One of the drivers saw me getting fuel and told me, "I've been with this company for ten years and haven't seen a truck this nice." So, he called in, and the company took it from me. I was still happy to be on my own and ended up with a brand-new truck.

The journey had begun. They gave me a load from Little Rock to Memphis, Tennessee. I dropped the load and went home to my family. I took everyone for a ride in my new company truck, and they loved it. I missed being home every night, but my life had just begun. I was home for four days and then had to roll.

My dreams had manifested right before my eyes. I had done it. Now was the time to study the business and take notes about everything I did. This was my time to shine. I never had a problem with asking for advice, because a closed mouth doesn't get service. No matter where I'm located, I ask questions. I have learned not to think I know it all, because there's still a lot to learn in trucking. So as long as I live, I won't take life for granted. Every day I wake up, I'm still in school.

> Hear, O my son, and receive my sayings;
> and the years of thy life shall be many. I
> have taught thee in the way of wisdom; I
> have led thee in right paths.
> (Proverbs 4:10–11)

Chapter 2

TRAVELING IS A BLESSING

How does it feel growing up in a place that has very little traffic? I wondered about this every day as I watched television and saw the beautiful blue ocean waters. Occasionally I would catch myself in a daydream about lying on the beach somewhere around the world. I always wondered what New York City looked like or what the White House in Washington DC looked like. Was it true that the White House looked like a big white castle? Was the water really blue like they showed it on TV? All those thoughts were going through my mind, but I always said that, if the Lord spared my life, I would travel to all forty-eight states as well as some out-of-country places before I leave this earth.

Traveling to a place I've never been to before has always been a blessing to me. When I am traveling with the windows down letting the fresh air blow over me, I feel as if that air is the Lord's breath, and that's the reason the air is so fresh. Sometimes when I am traveling I can drive from point A to point B with no problems. Every time I make it to a location or my destination I thank the Lord for his traveling mercy.

There are people all around the world, including myself sometimes, who don't acknowledge where our blessings come from, and who don't understand that we are taking our privileges for granted. What do I mean? For example, driving while we are tired. There have been many times I have been on the highway traveling, knowing I should have shut down. But I have kept driving, saying to myself that I can make it. Do you know how many people have lost their lives because drivers have continued to drive while they were tired? In my years of driving I have seen so many tractor-trailer accidents that were caused by drivers falling asleep behind the wheel. Truck driving is dangerous, and trucks are very hard to stop. If people only knew the impact of a truck hitting a car at normal speed! The truck can fold a car up like a hand can crumble up a piece of paper. If people did their research on tractor-trailers, they would respect the truck driver more. I respect the truck because, after having my first experience of not being able to stop when a car pulled out on me, I learned to be more cautious.

I really enjoy traveling on the road. I have a lot of time to think about all the things I will be dealing with before I get home, and by the time I make it home I know how to solve my problems. I've been traveling since I graduated high school in 2001. Some people think that traveling is boring, or maybe they feel that way because they have never been anywhere. I can understand if you're traveling to the same place every time you leave town. Now that could get a little a boring. Let's be mindful. Traveling is a blessing. It is a chance to get away from home and explore new places. Have you explored your home state? Have you been to the capital in your state? When we learn about the history of our home state we see that there is a lot we didn't know—so much that it would amaze every person. If you have never been outside of your town and you're able to travel, why not clear your schedule one weekend and explore your home state? Fill your car up with gas and choose somewhere you have never been. Your first journey will make you feel like going somewhere every chance you get.

I thank the Lord for this opportunity because there are so many people who can't travel on their own because they can't see, can't walk, and would love to trade places with you. Sometimes we take our positions for granted. Can you imagine having a career that forces you to sit behind a desk every day all day while your boss keeps getting on your nerves? "Can you do this when you finish? Can you handle that?" Imagine a boss whose favorite saying is something like this: "Hi. I don't mean to bother you, but after you're finished with what you're doing, can you do this little favor for me. I would appreciate it." Are you tired of sitting? I would be.

When I am behind the wheel of my truck, I can always stop, get out, and get something to drink or eat. That is what makes my job fun. Some people don't like to drive, but I love to drive. I know I was born with this desire because, ten years later, I still have a strong desire to drive a truck. I heard a song on the radio once called "Born to Ride," and all I could do was laugh.

I left home one Monday morning to pick up my load. I had a blowout on my way there. A blowout sounds like a grenade going off down the road. If you hear that sound, more than likely, one of your tires has blown out. I pulled over to do my walk-around to see which tire had blown. I was two exits away from my destination where I was to pick up my load. I notified my dispatcher to let him know what had happened. He asked me how close I was to the shipper, and I told him. He told me to be safe driving to the shipper and that he would send a tire guy to me. I did just that, but before I could get there, I drove by a Department of Transportation (DOT) inspector who was sitting in his car at the next exit. When I passed the exit, the DOT inspector saw my blown tire, and he put his lights on and pulled out to stop me. He said, "Sir, did you know you are riding on a blown-out tire?" He asked me for my license, registration, medical card, and logbook. I told him the truth and gave him everything he asked me for. He said, "Where are you headed?" I said, "I am one exit from where I pick up my load. I know about the tire. It blew a few miles back. My dispatcher told me to make it to the shipper to pick up my load, and while I'm waiting he'll have the tire guy come change the tire right there." The inspector said, "Okay, I'll be right back." He came back after everything I gave him checked out to be legal and said, "Sir, everything is okay." He gave me a warning for riding on a blown tire and let me make it to the shipper. I was so thankful. I had slipped through another obstacle safely without getting a ticket.

You see, some may say that it may have been luck that caused him to let me go, but I don't believe in luck. I believe either we are blessed for the cause or we are cursed for the cause. If you have had this experience in your life, and the cop or state trooper or DOT inspector has let you go without giving you a ticket, just know that the Lord was watching over you and covering you. Should this stop you from driving? No, of course not. But things like this are going to happen sometimes when you least expect them.

When I made it to the shipper and sat there waiting for the tire guy to come, I decided to take a nap. When I woke up, they were finished loading my truck, but the tire guy hadn't come yet to change my tire. I sat there for another hour, and he finally showed up apologizing to me and explaining why he was running behind. I told him I accepted his apology, but doesn't it get under your skin sometimes when you are ready to go and something else is keeping you from leaving?

I am sure we all have experiences like this one. This taught me patience. It made me even more humble. My favorite message of gratitude to the Lord is this: "Lord, thank you for keeping me and protecting me." You see, when we can't figure out why things are going the way they are going in our day, when we can't change what is happening, we should rest in the Lord. What I mean is that some things we can't control, so when we can't control them, we should understand that the Lord is protecting us from something else that could kill us. It can be one or two or many things. If you haven't been paying attention to what is going on while you are traveling, it is truly a blessing that someone this great is watching over you even when you are not thinking about watching over yourself. This is why traveling is a blessing.

> I call heaven and earth to record this day
> that I have against you, that I have set before
> you, life and death, blessing and cursing:
> therefore choose life that both thou and thy
> seed may live. (Deuteronomy 30:19)

Chapter 3

GETTING UP EARLY AND LYING DOWN LATE

S ometimes my schedule is so on point that I can cruise through the week with no setbacks. I am a person you might call an early bird—someone who gets up at two, three, or four o'clock in the morning to drive. I really love this time of morning because most people around the area I am in are still sleeping. When I get up this early, the first thing I do is drop down on my knees in front of my bed and magnify and glorify my heavenly Father. I thank him for letting me rise again to correct what I didn't get right the day before.

You see, I have learned that I can't bring yesterday's problems with me, so I have to accept what I am able to work with today. This is why getting up early is so important to me. I can have a one-on-one with my daddy (Lord) with no interruptions. He always gives me a response with a soft voice letting me know he hears me. The only distraction I have to deal with that early is Satan! He is always busy and loves to attack while we are sleeping. When I am finished meditating with my daddy, I grab my logbook and do what I need to fix it. Sometimes I've taken off without fixing it if I've overslept, and fixed it once I make it to the customer.

When I make it safely to my destination I say, "Lord, thank you for protecting me and getting me safely here." Getting up early makes me aware of how a person on the road might approach me as if his car has broken down and his wife and kids are still in the car. I've heard that line so many times it's what made me stop believing in them. We have to be careful out there because some people are not trying to do you right, and if they can get anything out of you, they will take it. I never let my window all the way down to answer questions, or open my door when I could be facing a trick or lie. You can't tell sometimes when people truly need help, but the only way to find out for yourself is sit back in your truck or whatever you are riding in and watch. This will teach you how to respond when you are approached.

Take, for example, an issue of a "broken down" car. Now,

I don't think my wife would let me leave her and my daughter in a disabled car while I hike three miles up the interstate to the city for help. We would stay together all the way. If anything happened while we were out together, the Lord would respond through prayer. He would send help because he always takes care of his children. His word tells me to place *all* my cares upon him. Say you are at a gas station and a man approaches you with the line, "Excuse me, sir, my car is broken down, and my wife and kids are in the car on the side of the interstate. I don't have any money. Can you help me?" You have to listen to the key words: *broken down*. You ask him, "What type of help do you need?" He says, "I'm out of gas." Now how can he have left out the fact that he is out of gas when he was explaining that he needed help and had left his wife and kids in the car? This person said "broken down," and a broken-down car needs more attention than gas. Let's say you give the guy $20 for gas and then buy him a gas can to put the gas in. Then you sit in your truck or car and you watch the man ask other people the same question he asked you. You will see that this person in need of "help" is really a hustler. If his story had been true, he would be rushing to get back to his family as soon as someone helped him out.

Let's get back to getting up early, something I still enjoy. When I get up early before rush hour starts, I always make it to my customer ahead of schedule, and a lot of times the customer accepts my load early. Even though I am a company driver, I operate my truck as an owner-operator would. When my dispatcher gives me a load, I plan my trip from point A to point B. I call the shipper and let them know that I am picking up a load, and I ask if I can load early. Sometimes the answer is yes and sometimes it's no. I make the same arrangements with the place where the load is going. When I know I'm going to be delivering to a particular place a lot, I call hoping to speak to the plant manager or transportation manager to build a relationship with him or her, just in case I make it late or need to be moved up. It helps to have a personal relationship. It's called "favor with the customer". If you are early in your daily task, more than likely you will get service because everyone loves to serve the early bird. I don't like to be late; it creates a bad name, especially if you are habitually late. You want a good name so that people will speak highly of you, and when the time comes for position or a favor, your name has already been ringing.

When you figure out how to deal with your job, you can use the information to work for you and not against you. I remember the time my dispatcher called and said, "Hey, Nelly!" (That was my nickname at the time.) "How did you get loaded and on the road four hours early?" I said,

"When we learn how to pull strings without breaking them, we will always be ahead." Sometimes people forget that, before truckers became truckers, they had a life of doing something else. We all came from doing something else that held our interest before we took up trucking. The thing we must do is implement our talents in our daily lifestyle, no matter where we learned them.

I never tell people that I am a truck driver because so many bad things have been said about truck drivers. Some people see me and can't believe that I drive a truck. I know it's how I carry myself and cater to myself. I dress in a casual, urban style, and I even switch it up sometimes and step out with a conservative look. If you saw me in a gas station or truck stop you would never guess that my job is behind the wheel of that big truck. You see, looks can be very deceiving. When a truck driver is early in everything he does, he always has a spot to park, a nice hot shower, a place to sit for a hot meal, and the majority of the time, an open fuel isle. This not only works with trucking; this also works if you have a desk job or are running your own business. I have figured out that, when I am early, I have more time to myself to enjoy. Otherwise, I find myself running right up to my time to deliver. I hate when I am out of time. That's why I love getting up early—so I can either be close to a customer or I can ride all day to my customer, which is also fine.

If I have fruit, juice, and something to snack on in the truck with me, I can run over 700 miles nonstop. It is legal for a trucker to drive 715 miles without any problems with the DOT. I have run harder than that when I'm trying to make it home. You are talking about somebody who is really amped when looking forward to seeing the smile on my wife and daughter's face. I did a run one time from Staten Island, New York, to Nashville, Tennessee, in less than twenty-four hours. That ride was 880 miles. I was not legal on my logbook.

I never speak about all these crazy things to my wife because she would worry about me while I am on the road. She is such a blessing to me. She enjoys what I do because I changed her mind about trucking when she went on the road with me. We had so much fun together, playing in the truck and eating together at the truck stops. Our favorite spot is the Petro restaurant. My wife and I both love the salad bar. The food is fresh, but sometimes the craziness of people who walk from outside and go straight to the salad bar and grab the same serving utensil that everyone else uses, bugs both my wife and me. This is why being home is important, where we are sure that everything is clean and we don't have to worry about getting behind someone who doesn't have clean habits.

When we're home on the weekend, I call the company

and plan my Monday morning pickup. You see, being on top of your game only positions you to greatness in everything you do. Why wait until Monday and sit around until noon because there is no load available when you can act like you're an owner-operator and be ahead of your week? Some truck drivers can be great dispatchers. The reason I am saying this is that truckers communicate face to face with the customers. We know the interstates because we are always on them, and we know what best to do when trouble strikes on the road.

I thank the Lord for this ability to serve, because we do more than just drive trucks. We serve the nation. I love to leave home at four o'clock on a Monday morning when my load is already ready. I never leave home without asking the Lord for traveling mercy on the road. We can't stop life from being life, but what we can do is ask for protection before trouble strikes. And if we think about how many times he has covered us, even when we weren't asking for anything, it should make us all feel some type of comfort that we are being watched over.

I remember one early morning when I was leaving Atlanta, Georgia, traveling Route 75 north toward Chattanooga, Tennessee. I was approaching the 75/85 split when, out of nowhere, a four-wheeler—in other words, a passenger car—on my right, crossed over into my lane, and

I had my first accident. When I hit the guy, I stabbed my brakes, and my trailer jackknifed and blocked all the traffic in the northbound lane of Route 75. Thank God there was no traffic on the interstate at the time this happened. The guy in the car was scared for his life, and I was scared for his life also. He had been driving while he was on the phone, and that was what caused the accident, but I thank God no one was hurt. I got out of the truck to check on the guy, and as soon as he saw me, he began to apologize. I told him that the main thing was that he was not hurt. I immediately called 911. We sat and waited for the trooper. Since no one was hurt, the trooper didn't arrive for almost an hour. Once he arrived, the guy told him that it was his fault for driving into my lane. The trooper wanted the guy and I to exchange contact and insurance information, and after that the trooper went back to his car. When he got back out of his car, he told the guy he could leave. The trooper told me to go sit in my truck.

I didn't think anything of it because I had never been in an accident before. After a while, I looked in my mirror and saw the trooper trying to get my attention. He was waving his hand for me to come to the back of the truck. I wasn't nervous at all until he said, "Mr. Milam, did you know that you are riding on a suspended license?" I said, "Are you serious?" He said, "Yes, and as of right now, you are under arrest." He read me my rights.

I remembered that I had paid a ticket late, and I wondered if that was why my license had been suspended. You see, the Lord gave the devil permission to intervene in the accident to stop me for my license. I was on my way up north to Portland Springs, Maine, where they were doing a level-three DOT inspection. If I had made it to Maine, my situation would have been a lot worse than what it was, so I was very thankful for the small accident. I spent my first-ever night in jail, in the downtown Atlanta County jail. You would be surprised how many people were in for driving on suspended licenses that night, riding with no tags, and driving with no insurance.

People are taking a risk every day to make it to and from work without getting pulled over, but that night the events were meant to happen. I stayed awake all night. The correction officer did me a favor that night and moved me to another cell away from everyone else. He said, "You don't look like you belong with this crowd." I said, "Thank you, sir. I'm here because I paid a ticket late and still got my license suspended, which is a lesson learned—to stay out of the fast lane so I won't have to worry about paying any tickets." While I was in jail, my company towed my truck back to the Nashville yard. I had to ride a Greyhound bus back home. My company paid the tow bill and my Greyhound ticket, and I thank the Lord that the judge waived all the fees and released me to go home so I could get my license straightened out. I was rolling again two weeks later. No matter what has happened in my life, nothing has made me frightened of trucking. I love trucking, and I like to roll. In fact, I still to this day enjoy getting up early and rolling. But some of the things that I have experienced could have been prevented if I had taken care of business when it happened. I think I will take my time now when traveling and make sure I am doing everything the right way. Hopefully this will minimize my troubles—I can't say all my troubles, but some.

> I waited patiently for the Lord; and he
> inclined unto me, and heard my cry. He
> brought me up also out of a horrible pit, out
> of the miry clay, and set my foot upon a rock
> and established my goings. (Psalm 40:1–2)

Chapter 4

PRAYING ALL AROUND THE CLOCK

Have you found yourself praying the whole day and you don't know why you are praying so much? What you do know for certain, however, is that prayer is the best thing going in your life, especially when you remember that the Lord has answered so many prayers.

Sometimes the Lord wakes me up earlier than usual and I lie there scratching my head trying to figure out why I am awake at one or two o'clock in the morning. Then it hits me—the Lord wants to fellowship with me. It's just as it is when your mom or dad or whoever you are staying with sometimes might sit at the end of your bed, and you see him or her when you wake up. This person might tell you that everything is okay, and that you should go back to sleep. "I am just thinking, that's all." The person probably really wants to talk. This is why the Lord wakes us up sometimes early in the morning. He wants to build an early-morning relationship with us.

You see, he taught me a lot of things—things I didn't learn from people. He is a teacher, and his word tells me that, when I seek him first, and also seek the kingdom of God and his righteousness, all will be added. I truly believe that his word is real because he has proven it to me many times in my life. I know that he is alive and well. A strong prayer life with the Father is a powerful relationship we all need. Without it we can be hurt in times of need. This is why I have learned to pray all day and all night. This is how I became a spiritual man. I am not religious about what I am doing, but I am relational with him about what I am doing.

When I get behind the wheel of a big truck, or even a car, I don't mind bowing my head in prayer before I travel because, even though I know that I am covered and protected through the blood of Jesus, I can still acknowledge him and let him know that I am thankful for traveling mercy. He waits to hear our voices every day as we acknowledge that we are blessed and that he is our guidance, and we will not be led without his presence in all that we do.

Are we thankful for what we have? Do we understand

that being able to see, being able to walk, and being able to touch and feel are very important abilities in our life? We need these abilities to go out into the world where we can reach the lost at all cost. We sometimes, as humans, act as if nobody is watching us. We really do not understand that we are all really held responsible for all we do. You see, when we don't pray, we don't build, and this handicaps us to the point that stress will arise over our lack of a prayer life.

Have you heard the saying "if you don't work you don't eat"? Well, that saying is real because, if you are an adult paying your own bills and providing for yourself, if you don't work you won't eat. This is why I love to pray, but when I was young and my family was bringing me up in the church, I didn't understand that I was going to need a prayer life for my entire life. The reason I talk with my Daddy all day is that I know he is my everything and my all. He was protecting me when I didn't want to bond with him or have a personal relationship him. He watched over me when the enemy was plotting to take my life. He still had mercy on me even when I heard the word and I still went out and did opposite of what he said to do, and he still loved me. When I dose off to sleep in my car or dose off to sleep in my truck, the Lord is my driver. When I am driving on black ice or in heavy rain and can't control my vehicle, the Lord is my driver. So, when I make it to my destination safely, I have to tell somebody what the Lord has done, even when they look at me as if I am crazy.

Some people don't pray and don't understand why prayer is important. They move like the wind back and forth and never have truly found their place in the Lord. I remember when I first prayed. It was difficult because I didn't know what to expect from God when I prayed. Prayer changed my mindset about a lot of things. Prayer made me humble. It made me think a lot more than usual. When I found out, in his word, that he already knew what I was going to be, praying about it blew my mind. I feel special to be connected to this type of power. I feel honored to be a chosen child of God and not a mistake. I pray because I know what kind of result I'm going to get from prayer.

You can be a young person or an older person, and prayer works the same. I don't suggest praying about things that are not realistic. I don't suggest taking it as a joke and mocking another person about how he or she prays. The only way to know if prayer works for you is try it for yourself. Trying it for yourself is the best teacher because you don't have any outside influences to tell you what to pray for. There are so many people who pray only when they are at church, but there is one prayer that everyone should know, and it is the only prayer that lets you know that your prayers are being answered. That is a sinner's prayer:

Lord, come into my life and save me. I
acknowledge that I'm a sinner, and I repent
for all that I have done. Lord, forsake all that
I have done. I totally surrender to your will.
Lord, forgive me for my sins. Come into my life
and save me. I believe by the confession of my
mouth and the commitment in my heart that
you died and rose for me. Lord, I receive your
salvation, and I believe by faith that I am saved.

You can't go wrong with this prayer. It makes you feel
better. When you look in the mirror, you might say, "Well,
I don't look better." But I am letting you know that, if you
just continue on in prayer, continue on in faith, and make
the Lord royalty in your life and not the minority in your
life, your looks will catch up with how you feel about God.
You see, anybody can pray, but when you pray and begin
to get results from what you are praying about, that makes
you want to continue praying to the Lord. We can pray all
day and night about a lot of things that we want and need,
but is that working out for you? Is what you are asking for
coming to pass?

I will praise the Lord according to his
righteous; and will sing praises to the name
of the Lord most high. (Psalm 7:17)

Chapter 5

CAN'T MAKE IT HOME FOR DINNER

How do you feel when you miss an important gathering or dinner when everyone is waiting for you? Do you make it up to the people you disappointed? I can remember so many times when I didn't make it home for dinner. I understood my job, but my wife was very upset a lot. Could I blame her for being mad when she did not understand what could happen? I couldn't imagine how she felt when she had cooked a dinner for her husband and I didn't show up until the next morning. I could feel, after this happened several times, that she was ready to call it quits, but she loved me and waited it out. She said to me she figured that, if we were going to be together, she had to learn my life.

She came to me one day very upset about her job. I had listened to complaint after complaint for some time. So, I said to her, "I have checked out all your bills, and I can handle them. You can roll with me to learn what I do." I said, "Look at it this way: your bills will be paid, and we can travel the world together." I said, "What do you say? I know your job is stressing you out." She paused for a long time while she looked at me. I had my hands in my pockets with my fingers crossed. I said, "There's nothing wrong with a change of scenery." She said that she needed a little time, and I said, "Take all the time you need." After that conversation, I never brought it back up, but I thought that eventually—hopefully—one day she would change her mind.

One Friday evening I made it home early, and she was sitting in her car in the driveway. She called to me, and I got into her car with her. She was crying, and that touched my heart because she is so beautiful to me, and I didn't want to see her sad. I said, "Calm down and tell me what's wrong."

She said, "I am having an affair." I said, "An affair?" And my head went down. I was crushed, and I covered my face. She said, "Baby, I am just playing with you! I quit my job!"

We both laugh about it now, but I was still feeling emotional at the moment, and she said, "I am serious. I quit my job today."

I said, "Come here," and I hugged her and told her that it would be okay and that I had her back. I was very pleased to see she was going to trust me to have her back. I kept my word then, and today I can say, seven years later, that I am still keeping my word.

When Monday came around, we hit the highway together. I tell you, I was a happy little camper. I mean I was so happy to have my soul mate on the road with me, and she began to see with her own eyes why I sometimes couldn't make it home on time. I said, "Thank you, Lord, for making my prayer come to pass."

I really always tried hard to make it home on time, but rush-hour traffic put the brakes on me every time. There are many situations that keep people from getting home to their families, but we have to keep on communicating to them about why we can't make it. There have been times when I've sat in traffic for three or four hours because of a highway accident and I've had to call home to cancel our date. After my wife saw all the incidents that I had to face every day, she apologized to me because she understood what was going on out there.

She didn't go with me every time, and that's when distractions always messed with my wife's mind. You see, Satan comes to steal, to kill, and to destroy. He comes to steal your joy, kill your drive or motivation, and destroy your peace with yourself and everything that you love. One incident I remember happened in Newburgh, New York. My wife and I were rolling on Interstate 84 west when all of a sudden my radiator burst and the fluids covered my windshield. I pulled over. I raised the hood and saw my problem. Oil was everywhere. I called a wrecker service in the area to come tow my truck. The wrecker guy was very nice to us, and he let us borrow his car for a day so we could get back and forth while they worked on my truck. Everything happened for a reason. My wife had told me to stop and take a break, but I had insisted on driving. I said, "Baby, please. When we get back home, we'll fly to Atlanta and go shopping."

She said, "Great. But you've been driving all the way here to deliver, and now you're going to drive all the way home with no break."

I said, "I'm amped up and ready to get home."

The reason this happened was that the Lord was saving my life by keeping me out of a bad accident. I could see it after lying in bed in the motel room for a day, and I felt really tired. People think things just happen, but I know things don't just happen without a reason. When you are traveling down the highway and a situation occurs with your vehicle, do you beat yourself up? Do you feel like everything bad keeps happening to you? Do you think, why can't I get a break? What is wrong with me?

We ask a lot of question when trouble strikes, don't we? But why don't we ask a lot of questions when trouble doesn't strike?

If you're a person who travels for a living and have a family at home, it would be a great thing to sit them down and communicate with them about some of the things that delay your return home. Keeping them in the dark can cause a lot more problems than we think. Save your relationship, save your marriage. Don't be the person who comes home only to pay the bills and then hits the road again. This person has no life unless he or she is living the life on the go and is cool with his or her relationship. I love going to work and coming home to a beautiful wife and child. I love being greeted with a nice hot bubble bath and a hot meal that puts me to sleep.

So, we discovered that many things keep us from returning to our destination on time. I thank the Lord for a wife like mine, and I know she is thankful for a husband like me.

> Live joyfully with the wife whom thou
> lovest all the days of the life of thy vanity,
> which he hath given thee under the sun, all
> the days of thy vanity: for that is thy portion
> in this life, and in thy labor which thou
> takest under the sun. (Ecclesiates 9:9)

Chapter 6

MY DESTINATION IS COMING UP

I t was three in the morning in Milford, Connecticut. I felt as if I was the only person up, but I knew someone else was up with me. It always feels good sleeping in my bed in my truck when the motor is running because the motor vibrates the entire truck. This puts me in mind of sitting on my grandmother's knee as she rocked me to sleep. When I finally pulled myself together that morning, I sat there and looked around at all the pretty lights on the other rigs. I closed my eyes and thanked the Lord for waking me up for another blessed day. I fixed my logbook, turned on my hazard lights, and then got out of the truck to do my pre-trip inspection. During this inspection, the person who is operating the truck walks around the vehicle checking everything on the truck from the front to the back of the trailer, making sure that there are no leaks on the ground and that all the lights are working properly. I can also do this pre-trip inspection while fueling my truck at the fuel isle.

Every time I came to Milford, I had to eat at Wendy's. I thought I was going to turn into chicken nuggets. After I got my food and a nice cold Mountain Dew, I was ready to roll. I like to roll out early in the morning because the only people up are the early birds. Hopefully the roads are clear from any accidents or roadwork. You can roll the way you want too without having to deal with those issues. We still have to be careful because the state troopers are always working. We call them bears on the CB.

My CB handle is First Mile. First Mile has put in over a million miles, and I am so thankful for the Lord's mercy and grace, which is what has got me this far. If you are up driving any time from midnight to five o'clock in the morning, you will see that it is a peaceful and pleasant time to roll because no one is on the highway. While everyone is asleep, and the phone is not ringing, this is a perfect time to commune with the Father. As I arrived at my destination in Poland Springs, Maine, I began to thank my Lord for helping me make it safely to another destination.

Do you think you made it to your destination without any distraction all by yourself? If you set your alarm and you woke up when it rang, who do you think woke you up to hear the alarm? Have you ever thought to yourself, why am I still here? Have you ever thought that it could've been you when you saw someone else in the ditch? I know you might feel as if you can get through anything without prayer or you have tried prayer and it's not working. I know it feels strange sometimes to try some things that we have never tried before. I feel good when I open my mouth and talk to my Father because he answers my prayers. If you don't believe what I believe, but you do believe in a Higher Power or a Higher Resource, I want you to say, "Higher Power, I don't understand what I am doing, and I want to trust you, but I don't know you, and I want to know you. I can see that I could've been dead, but I'm still here. If you hear me, I ask that you lead and guide me and help me make the right choice by reaching out to you."

Even when we don't understand that sometimes the choices we make put us in a bind, we keep making the same choices. Even when we think we don't have the faith to do some things or to go to a destination, we believe we will get there. A destination is a place to which someone or something is being sent. A destination is also a place that people will make a special trip to visit. How do you feel when you reach your destination? I can travel in a car, a plane, a train, or a tractor-trailer to get to my destination. I can even walk or jog to my destination, but getting there takes some action. At four in the afternoon, when I was fixing my logbook to head back south out of Poland Springs, Maine, I know I heard a voice just as clear as a bell. This voice was from the Lord, and he said, "Don't leave your destination until six o'clock." I don't listen to this voice every time, and I didn't this time, but this voice was right, and I should have listened. I pulled out of the customer's lot in Poland Springs at four, and when I made it to the toll booth, I encountered the DOT inspector who was right on the other side of the toll booth. You see, the Lord didn't tell me why I shouldn't leave, but if I had waited, I wouldn't have got stopped by our friends in blue. They were waiting all along, and the Lord knew it. He was trying to protect me the whole time. Because I hadn't listened and obeyed the Lord's command, I was put out of service until I got a steering tire put on.

I thank the Lord again for protecting me. It is amazing to know that, when you have someone to call on or to talk to all day and commune with all week, you have a blessing. He has never let me down, either before or after I became a believer and a follower of my Lord and Savior Jesus the Christ.

In everything give thanks: for this is the
will of God in Christ Jesus concerning you.
(1 Thessalonians 5:18)

Chapter 7

HONEY, I'M HOME

W hat a wonderful feeling to make it home at a decent time. We all work long hours on the job sometimes, and I feel as if I am always on the clock. But when I see my gorgeous wife and daughter's face, the joy and happiness I get changes my whole day.

When I was a young man I always watched family movies with my grandmother. In one movie I watched the wife cooking dinner while the kids were running around the house. When the husband came home from work, everyone rushed to the door to meet "Dad" when he opened the door. I wondered to myself if that would ever happen to me one day, and then I grew up and was blessed with my own family. So, the movie I had watched came to pass for me.

When I come into the house now, my wife and daughter meet me at the door with hugs and kisses. I feel like a king. All my worries fly out the door. The fast pace comes to an end for the time being, and I can rest. I feel special to have someone waiting for my return. There are people who say they love being by themselves, but in their minds I know they want to be loved by someone special. It wasn't meant for man and woman to be alone; this was established in the beginning of time.

When I pull up outside my home, I can smell that seasoning from the inside of my house. My wife can really put it down in the kitchen. She cooks like she is in love, and I eat like I am making love to the food. I call my wife Cheforkee. My home is my sanctuary. Walking into my home is like leaving the world for a moment and walking into a place of peace. My wife loves to hear me say, "Honey, I'm home!" And my daughter says, "Daddy!" And then she jumps into my arms.

Are you so consumed with work that you don't see your significant other? Are you working so many hours that, when you do get home, you just want to sleep and never enjoy your significant other, but while you are at work you are turned up to the max? I know some of us are single and would love to come home to someone who has already cooked dinner and put the kids to bed.

Or maybe you just want to come home to a hot dinner because you don't have kids and don't want kids. I want to be loved, and my wife proves to me that she is happy with me loving her.

Sometimes when it's time to leave for work, I don't want to leave my wife and daughter because of the love they show me and the love I give them. That's why it's so hard to leave. If you are a person who has no family and who works all the time and you love being on the road, how do you enjoy your life with no one to share it with? Have you been hurt to the point that you don't want anybody in your life? Or is it that you were raised in a home where you were embarrassed so deeply that you couldn't be yourself?

There are plenty of reasons that we sometimes want to be alone. I know when I wanted to be alone it was because I felt hurt. I wanted to find myself, but it took a while because of the pain. So, I understand when someone wants to be alone for that reason. You may have had a bad experience in your life in a relationship when you were working long hours on the clock and not spending enough time at home. This sort of situation can sometimes push people into an unfaithful status. If we don't communicate or educate our loved one on what we do at our job, the resulting lack of understanding can hurt our relationship. So many relationships don't make it because couples don't sit down and talk this kind of thing out with one another, and one day it just blows up and everybody calls it quits.

I truly believe in second chances to get it right, but first we must get ourselves together before we bring others into our lives. The first thing we need to do is ask the Lord for forgiveness, and then we must forgive ourselves. Once we have healed from the hurt, we must get ourselves in position to receive our new love. I believe everyone wants to come home to a companion who has been chosen by the Lord. I remember the day I was ready for my wife. I said, "Lord, you know my heart. I am a faithful driver, and I am ready for you to send me a faithful wife who loves you first. Because, if she loves you first, and she is for me, she won't have a problem with loving me." He answered my prayers. You see, when you get yourself together for him, he will deliver to you the right package—your soul mate. When you open up to your soul mate, you will feel as if you have hit the lottery. But it won't be the lottery; it will be a blessing that you have been patiently waiting for.

Patience is not just for the person at home waiting for you to get off work; it's for you also to do your job correctly and then get home to your family safely. When you have been at work for over ten hours and you are ready to go home, your homecoming will be so much nicer and so much happier when you have someone to come home to.

> Be patient therefore, brethren, unto
> the coming of the Lord. Behold, the
> husbandmen waiteth for the precious fruit
> of the earth, and hath long patience for it,
> until he receive the early and latter rain.
> (James 5:7)

Part II

RESTING

Chapter 8

NO STRESS: ALL THE BILLS ARE PAID

D oes it feel great to know that all your bills are paid and are paid on time? What a relief of pressure when you are scrambling to pay that final notice and you make the exact date they are supposed to cut service.

Every Thursday night at midnight, my paycheck is directly deposited into my account, so the money is there when I wake up on Friday morning. The bank has it set up now so I can get an e-mail on my phone when the deposit hits my account.

Who handles the bills at your house? Are you always on time to pay your bills? Or do you wait until you get the final notice in the mail before you make payment? If you wait until the last minute with your bills, that is an indication that you probably wait until the last minute to do almost everything. If we look at our lives and examine the way we do a lot of things, we will see that we were not taught some important good habits as we were growing up. The reason is that those who raised us hadn't been taught certain things either, and they had to learn on their own. I don't care how holy you are, when the bills are due and your wife is in your ear and nothing is going right at that moment, a little stress seems to ease in.

We are living in a world where it's not just old people who have high blood pressure; rather, young people are experiencing this problem too. One main reason for this is stress. And a lot of stress comes from how people are going to pay their bills.

When you are lying on your couch or in your bed and you know that everything is paid, it makes you feel on top of the world for a moment. Nobody can say anything to you to get you upset unless you let them take you to that place. Do you pay your own bills? If you do, you may ask questions like these: Why can't I get ahead? Why, after I pay my bills, is there nothing left? Have I checked myself lately on my spending and what I am spending my money on besides essentials? Why can't I ever go out of town? Why do I have to work all the time? What strategy am I using to save money? Do I have too many bad habits, and is that the reason I can't go forward? Do I need help?

Sometimes we are so busy in our daily tasks that we don't stop to look at our own surroundings. You may ask yourself questions like these: When was the last time I took a day off work and catered to myself? When was the last time I turned the music down when I got in the car to go to work, so I could have a moment of silence on my way? Why can't we make ends meet even though we are two people who both have jobs?

When two incomes are coming into the home, there should be no stress if you are living within your means. Your home should have peace like no other place. When we follow the correct guidelines in taking care of business, everything will fall into place. I have seen happiness like no other when everything is paid on time at my house. Do you know the joy your wife experiences when she knows that she is protected? Husbands can feel the same joy when they know their wives are contributing!

It is a wonderful feeling to know that you are leading and providing for your family. Just knowing that you have extra money left in the account after everything is paid for the month should make you want to jump for joy. Everyone can't jump for joy. Because of poor managing, some people don't have money left over. Until they come to a place in life where they can sit down to rethink how they want to live, this will keep happening.

Some people stand all day at work, and while they are standing they are thinking about what they are going to do when they get off work. Sometimes their plans don't involve taking care of important business at home. This can happen because they are standing. People who sit down all day at their jobs, especially in front of a computer with internet access, have a little more leverage to take care of business at home than someone who has to stand all day. If you are not taking advantage of this, then you are the problem.

I had to learn to manage my money a little better because I love shoes, and every pair of shoes I bought put me in the doghouse the next week. But over and over I bought them anyway. I needed some help with managing my money. It wasn't that I didn't seek financial help. I had an addiction that made me want certain things. I was just like someone addicted to any drug. I needed deliverance from the Lord. I got down on my knees and began to pray to the Father about my addiction. I said, "Lord, I need help. I come as boldly and as humbly as I know how to say that I need you. I am tired of repeating the same problem week after week. I work too hard. I put in seventy hours a week in a truck, and I come home and have nothing left by Monday. This has to stop. I have a child. I need to save for her to go to college. I need to sit down with someone to talk about retirement and how I want to live and how much I need for retirement."

It's okay to call out for help. This help can be from a financial adviser or it can come through spiritual obedience. I prefer spiritual obedience because, once you are delivered from a thing and you continue to thank the Lord and ask him to keep you, you will forever keep your deliverance through obedience. We can try everything on our own, and if we do it on our own, it will not last long, but we can do all things through him who strengthens us. I am stress free because of obedience. My home is in order, the bills are paid, and my loved ones are happy with me. So, we must put the Lord first in everything we do. We must also be a blessing to our fellow neighbors as the Lord is a blessing to us. In this way we will continue to be on top. I thank the Lord for helping me get my priorities together. With his help I will forever succeed.

God is faithful, by whom ye were called
unto fellowship of his son Jesus Christ our
Lord. (I Corinthians 1:9)

Chapter 9

NEVER GET OUT OF YOUR TRUCK

t was three in the morning. I was parked in a customer's parking lot in Harrisburg, Pennsylvania, and I was sleeping when I heard a loud knock at my door. I lay there to see if I would hear it again. I heard it again, and that's when I got up. A guy was standing there acting as if something was really wrong. He said, "Help. Please help me. I am hurt."

I pulled myself together and wiped my eyes. I sat there in the driver's seat for a minute putting my shoes on, and then I started to open the door. But my angels said, "Don't get out. Roll down the window."

I rolled down the window far enough to hear the guy talk. I said, "What happened, sir?" He said to me that his wife and kids were in the car trapped. He had wrecked his car in his neighborhood, which was nearby, and he needed me to come help him pull them out. I thought about getting out of the truck for a second, but that feeling in my stomach would not leave. Then the guy got very impatient and climbed up on the side of the truck as if he wanted to break in. I rolled the window back up. There were other trucks parked in the lot with me, but the guy hadn't gone to the other trucks.

You see, if I hadn't listened to my angels telling me not to get out of the truck, I probably wouldn't be here to tell this story today. Thinking about everything that happened at three o'clock on that morning made me thank the Lord for his protection. Sometimes when we are not aware we make some real bad decisions in our lives, but the Lord covered me on that particular morning.

First of all, this guy said he'd had a wreck in his own neighborhood. I assume that each of us, in our own neighborhood, would know someone who could help us in a panic situation. We wouldn't have to run for help to a nearby distribution center where truckers are parked. We have to be very careful when it comes to panic situations when we are away from home. People can be very persuasive when they want what they want. Never get out of your vehicle when you are in a place that you are not familiar with when a stranger cries for help. I will tell anybody to think before opening his or her door.

The reason I am able to help someone else is that I heard a voice, and I obeyed this voice, and today I am so thankful. The enemy is Satan, and he comes to destroy human nature any way he can. He is a liar. He can be very smooth until he gets you to a place of no return. He doesn't come like a monster anymore. He wears the best clothes and the best shoes to trick you. He can be male or female, and he talks in such a way that his words are convincing. The cologne or perfume that he wears draws us in.

Are you risking your life picking up everyone you see who needs a ride just to say you did a good deed? Why take the risk if you have not heard the voice? One mistake can cost you your life. I am not saying that we shouldn't be mindful about helping people in need; what I am saying is that, in a situation like I was in, we need to carefully think about helping someone out if we are by ourselves, unless we have heard the voice from above.

"Though I walk through the valley of the shadow of death, I will fear no evil; for thou art with me, thy rod and thy staff they comfort me" (Psalm 23:4). We don't have to worry because we have a protector who protects his own. I look back at my life and realize there have been many experiences that could have caused my death. Has your life ever flashed right before your eyes? Have you ever opened your door to an unannounced caller and then wished you hadn't opened the door? Have you ever had that funny feeling in your stomach as if something is wrong? That funny feeling in your stomach is letting you know not to do something. Do you leave your house doors unlocked because you live in a gated area? Do you leave your car doors unlocked when you go into grocery stores? Sometime people watch your every move. That's why we have to be more careful how we move around.

One night while I was sleeping in my truck, the motor cut off by itself. I woke up very cold. The truck wouldn't turn back on. I got out with my flashlight to see if there were any leaks on the ground, but there were no leaks. I was confused, so I sat back in the truck, scratching my head. I turned the ignition switch off again, waited ten seconds, and then turned it back on. The truck just continued to turn over but would not start. I was parked among a lot of trucks, and I thought the only thing I had not checked was my fuel tanks. I got out to check them, and that's when I noticed that they were empty. I had fueled my truck about five hours earlier. Someone had stolen my fuel. I had to report to the company I was with at the time. I am so glad that I don't sleep with my windows down or sleep with my doors unlocked because this could have been more dangerous than it was.

Whether we are home or traveling, there are many reasons we should not just open our door. A person might know your name or sound very persuasive, but we shouldn't open up until we know for sure. We need to teach our young people about these things because they are going to be on their own one day, and they should know what to do and what not to do. Sometimes locks and other precautions don't stop intruders from entering, but we don't need to give them a free walk-in situation to our homes or cars. Waking up at gunpoint can be scary. Coming down your stairs in your home to see someone trashing your living room can also be very frightening. All these things can happen if we don't handle ourselves properly. Yes, the Lord is our protector, but he also has given us a calming sense that enables us to be mindful of doing our part. I thank the Lord for watching over me while I am asleep and keeping me safe on and off the road. I thank him for protecting my loved ones while I am away from them. I don't think people understand that the Lord has angels watching over them even when they think that the actions of these angels can be called luck. I don't believe in luck. I believe we are blessed or cursed. In every trial we encounter we must be thankful for the experience because, without experiences, how can we help someone else?

The thief cometh not, but for to steal, and to kill, and to destroy: I am come that they might have life, and that they might have it more abundantly. (John 10:10)

Chapter 10

TREAT EVERY TRIP LIKE A VACATION

Transportation has its pros and cons. You take each bad day as a learning experience. On the good days, you deliver your load and have no other load to pick up that day. This is where the fun comes in. Treat every trip like a vacation. You have the rest of that day to yourself. Why be upset that you didn't make it home when you can take home on the road with you? Sometimes you run out of time to park your truck in a good spot so you have to make the best out of that situation. When you get upset because you have to stay overnight, you only depress yourself. But you can make your bad thoughts into good thoughts.

I always find a Walmart or a mall to go to where I can

find out what's going on in the city I'm in. You can find out where to go to have a nice dinner by yourself. If you have your loved ones with you, that makes your trip even better! You may wonder how I move around in a city when I can't move my tractor-trailer. I just call a taxi to my location, and I can go where I want to go. This is how you can treat yourself while you are out of town and still be on the clock making money. If I park at the mall, I take a walk around the mall because I love to window shop. People don't understand that sometimes, when you don't have the money, you still can have experience of seeing what someone else may never see.

Do you tell yourself that you are blessed when you come into a place, blessed coming out of a place and blessed in the city you are in? Many will look upon you and see that you are blessed when you claim you are highly favored by God. It is truly a blessing to be at work and be taking a vacation at the same time. On one hand you are making money, and on the other hand, you are taking care of business while you travel.

Summertime has rolled in. The kids are out of school, and they need a getaway. Everyone is excited about going on the truck. We have everything we need to be comfortable. Have you ever been on a family vacation? There is so much to do when you are on a vacation. If you plan your trip before you leave home, you will not have any problems enjoying your family when you get to where you are going. Do you have to leave town to go on a vacation? Why can't an itinerary be created right there in your city or town, unless you live in a very small place that doesn't offer anything to do. I love to travel. I love to look up vacation destinations online because I always have said that, when I make it, I will be traveling a lot. I told my teacher in the first grade that I wanted to travel for a living. When she asked me what type of traveling, I told her I wanted to own my own trucking company. She told me that, if I did, I would go all over the world. It's true—I have been to a lot of places.

It excites me every time I am able to treat myself and my loved ones to a new place. I have been able to see the looks on their faces, and I get the same expression the first time I go to a place. When you take a vacation day and don't leave town, do you do something spontaneously that makes you feel as if you are out of town on a vacation? A small vacation can be anything you put together. You can first start out with dinner in a restaurant, and then go see a movie that's playing. After the movie, you make it home and take a short walk to think about the wonderful night you had. This is a vacation. Do you know what meditation is? Can you travel without leaving home? I travel all the time while I'm sitting on my couch in my living room. I travel in my mind! Can you imagine going back to a place that you have been to or have taken your family to? Meditation takes you where you want to go.

Meditating on the Word of God is the strongest form of traveling. His word takes you everywhere you want to go. Do you treat yourself in the physical realm? Do you treat your mind in the spiritual realm? How are you staying at peace with yourself? We have to learn to treat ourselves and stop waiting on people to treat us. When I close my eyes and meditate, I can go all over the country without leaving the house. This is some vacation I am having in my mind! When our minds are right, we can travel.

I treat myself every day to a passage from the Bible. How do we treat our loved ones? How do we treat our neighbors? Are we lining up with the word of God? Do we understand the word *treat*—not *trick-or-treat*, but treat? We can treat ourselves to a great setting only when our minds and hearts are in the right place. When someone tells you that the Lord said he wants to bless you, take it as the truth. I was a giver, and I never expected to receive anything back from anyone. I just gave from the heart. I never thought about being in a situation in which someone wanted to bless me. I didn't know if I should just take it. But after I studied and learned God's word, I learned to be humble about the blessings that someone else gave me. I love to treat myself, and these experiences have given me the drive to treat others and talk to others about exciting things I've experienced.

> I will meditate in thy precepts, and have
> respect unto thy ways. I will delight myself
> in thy statues: I will not forget thy word.
>
> (Psalm 119:15–16)

Chapter 11

BREAKER ONE NINE

"**B**reaker one nine" is something we say to another driver on the CB radio. We might also say, "Breaker breaker. Come on." When we say this, we are trying to get someone who is on the CB to answer, and once someone answers, you can communicate. Sometimes we ask for directions. Sometimes we just want to hold a conversation with anybody who will talk. You would be surprised what people on the CB talk about. If you thought that racism doesn't exist, you would find out really fast that it still does. The things people say to each other sometimes are uncalled for. I have heard a lot of bad things from other people. I love to help people when I can, and now since I know who I am, I don't mind accepting help too.

One day I had the CB up for a long period of time—longer than usual. A guy said, "Breaker one nine. Breaker one nine. This is Black and Grey. Does anybody copy?"

I said, "This is First Mile. What's your twenty? Come on." ("What's your twenty" means what is your location; "come on" means answer me!) He said that he'd received an e-mail on his Qualcomm that there had been an accident at exit 20 going westbound. He asked if there was another way to get around this traffic. I said, "Yes, sir, if you haven't passed the exit yet, you can get off on the Covington exit and take 385 south until you come to 240 west. That will take you to 40 west and back on track.

He said, "I copy that, First Mile. I appreciate the info. I'm trying to make it to west Memphis to exit 4 to get a parking spot before it fills up, if you copy?"

I said, "I copy. If you follow the directions I gave you to west Memphis, you'll touch down if there aren't any more hang-ups to stop you."

He said, "I copy that, First Mile. Enjoy the rest of your day."

"Right back at you, Black and Grey," I said. "You have a blessed journey and enjoy the rest of your night."

As we continue to travel on this journey called life, everyone we meet in our lives is not going to be polite to you. If your mother and father didn't teach you about how people will respond to you, sometimes these responses will get under your skin. Even when we are nice to people, they may not respond the way we want them to. There are some hateful people traveling these highways every day when we hit the road. We have to be mindful and responsible for our actions while we travel. The reason that people are hateful and resentful sometimes is that they hold on to things in their past that keep them from their future. So, the only way they can respond is to stay mad at the world.

I was talking to a lady one day for about half an hour. I told her that I was so happy that God had taken hate and anger out my heart. Her eyes immediately turned red. I said to myself, "Did I say something wrong or did I offend her?" I said to her, "Ma'am, what's wrong?" She dropped her head, and I said, "Do you believe in God?"

She said, "Yes, I did at one point, but now I don't know." She said, "Why did God take my only child?" I knew then she was mad at God, but she didn't understand that this same God who allowed her child to be taken had awakened her that morning.

We will always have questions that may never be answered until we meet the King, but until then I am going to keep believing and trusting him. Can we trust all the advice that people give us? Of course not. People will lead you down the wrong path, even when they know they don't know where to send you when you ask them for directions. How can someone do such a thing? Why do people lie in your face while looking you straight in your eyes? How can you send a person down a road knowing the road is a wrong turn? What's going on in your mind? What's your twenty? The Lord said to Adam, "Where art thou?" (Genesis 3:9). This means where are you? Why are you not in a position to be blessed and to be a blessing? Why didn't you help the homeless guy standing at the corner when you were sitting at the light with more than enough money to help him get a meal? Where are you? What are you thinking about? What drives you to help some people and not to help other people? Do you help people only when you're feeling great about yourself? Have you looked in the mirror lately? Do you understand your position? There is a position with your name on it. Now you might say, "Well, if this position has my name on it already, then I don't need to do nothing but wait for it." Sometimes in life that is true, but while we are waiting for things to happen in our lives, we must keep our minds at ease by learning to serve.

"Breaker one nine, can anybody hear me?"

"First Mile, once I get in position to be blessed and to be a blessing, then what?"

"You will accept the free gift once you are in position, but if you are a person who has tried every religion and still is not happy with your Breaker one nine/ position/ location, you must accept this gift: "For the Lord so loved the world, that he gave his only begotten Son, that whoever believeth in him should not perish, but have everlasting life (John 3:16). This is how you accept and receive the ultimate gift—by believing that your position is to be part of the body of Christ.

I have come a long way in my walk with Christ. I didn't understand my position at first, but the Lord taught me. He showed me the way to go and that my Breaker one nine is to stay connected and stay in position with his word. That way, I will not be tossed to and fro like the waves in the sea. Now, when someone is talking to you about a job or trying to get directions to a location, or if they ask you where are you living, that is a different breaker one nine, but when we are trying to determine our breaker one nine/position/ location with the Lord, we must know without a doubt that our breaker one nine is compatible with where we will spend eternal life.

> For ye have need of patience, that after ye
> have done the will of God, ye might receive
> the promise. For yet a little while, and he
> that shall come will come, and will not
> tarry. (Hebrews 10:36–37)

Chapter 12

TRUCKING IS A CAREER

What are your goals in life? Have you set any goals to accomplish this year? Every year around December people say that their New Year's resolution will be to stop doing something that they have been doing all the year before, or to start doing something. We can accomplish anything when we put our minds to it. We can do all things through him who gives us strength. Your accomplishment could be anything from stopping smoking and drinking to walking more and drinking more water. Your accomplishment can be starting the year off right by finding a church home.

One of the main reasons we don't accomplish a particular thing is that we don't keep our minds on the goal. We must write our visions down if we want to succeed with them. My understanding from research is that 90 percent of the people who write their plans or visions down succeed in what they plan. People who only say they are going to do something never do it because they never wrote anything down.

Do you have a career? Do you own your own business? Does the place where you are working have you covered if anything were to happen to your job? Do you have another job or financial security if the doors of your current employer were to close today? Ask yourself these questions: Am I okay with the pay? Am I secure if something were to happen at my job? Am I protected if I get hurt on the job? Does my company have another location where I could work if something were to happen? Do I have enough breaks for the workload I do? Am I working mandatory hours without any breaks? Am I protecting my future for being here? Have I ever set a goal in my life, and was I successful with it?

A career is not just a job; it is a backbone. When you can move in and out of the country, and your job is still needed, that's a career. How are you expecting to be the firefighter you always talked about if you never looked into what it is going to take to be a firefighter? How are you going to be a police officer if you never do the research so you know how to become qualified? When I was a kid in the first grade, my teacher, Mrs. Smart, asked all of us students what we wanted to be when we grew up! When it came time for me to answer, I said that I wanted to own my own trucking business. She said to me, "What kind of trucking business?" I said, "transportation business." She said, "Mr. Milam, if you do that, you will travel the world and see a lot of places."

I was excited because my uncles had their own trucking business. I didn't understand it enough at first because I was just in the first grade, but I knew a lot about what I already had seen. I watched my uncles do the job, and I would see trucks pass on the interstate every day. These experiences made me want to own my own company. One of my uncles said to me one day, "Little boy, you are not going to drive trucks. You are too little." I said, "Yes, I will when I get big like you."

You see, I made my mind up when I was younger what I wanted. But this choice doesn't have to be just for young people. An older person can make a decision in his or her mind to do something. I set a goal to go into the transportation industry. I made a commitment in my heart that I would drive a truck. When we put our minds and hearts into doing anything, it is more likely we will succeed. Those who only think about doing something, but never make a move, are not likely to be successful. The heart of a person reveals the truth every time. I say this because I know that we can say something to ourselves or just in general when we are speaking to someone and really not mean what we say because our heart is really not in it. The Lord said that people draw close unto him with their mouths, honor him with their lips, but their hearts are far from him. (Matthew 15:8). For example, say you were eating with some friends or colleagues, and one of your friends in your group observes that you all have been spending a lot of money on lunch and drinks every day. He or she suggests that you all contribute half of the money you are spending together and feed the homeless every day. Everyone agrees and says that would be a great idea, but weeks and weeks pass by, and no one brings the idea back up. This thought never made it to their hearts; we know this because they never fed the homeless.

Can a person speak and sound totally serious about doing something and then never act on what he or she said? Are you satisfied with your job title? Have you really sat back to see where you are in your life? If food supplies stop coming to the local grocery stores, what would you do? Do you want to continue to be the product in life or become the supplier of the product in life? A career is everything. I know right now that, if I keep my commercial driver's license (CDL) clean, I can move around every day of the year and have a job in the transportation industry. This is a career in which you can move anywhere in the country—and out of the country—and have a job already lined up before you move there. I am very thankful for my career, which the Lord has given me. I love my occupation—or should I say my profession. I feel very special to know that I am part of an industry that needs my occupation. Without the trucking industry, the world would stop. For example, let's say that a plane flies from point A to point B to deliver what's on the plane. We all know that a plane can't load or unload at Walmart, so we know a truck must deliver to Walmart. Ask yourself, does the world need your occupation? We need water, clothes, food, hygiene supplies, and so on. Are you working in an industry that needs your support? The world needs firefighters, it needs police, it needs nurses, and doctors. There are a lot of careers out there that are needed throughout the world. The world needs you! Are you going to sit and complain about your situation or make you situation a reality? We've got to move our feet when we say we are going to doing something with our lives, because we owe everything to ourselves first before we can help anybody else. We can't continue to be just talkers and not doers. Those who are *doing* something are moving forward; those who are not doing anything are not moving forward. If we're going to become anything successful in life, we must be both talkers and doers. Only then will we prosper.

And that he may run that readeth the Lord answered me, and said write the vision, and make it plain upon tables, it. For the vision is yet for an appointed time, but at the end it shall speak, and not lie: though it tarry, wait for it; because it will surely come, it will not tarry. (Habakkuk 2:2–3)

Chapter 13

GOING THE WRONG WAY

C an two people meet and fall head over heels for each other at first site? Say that two people really love each other and respect each other's feelings, but the problem is that one believes in God and the other doesn't. If they are basing their relationship on moral values, it can work, but once this couple begins to see if their relationship lines up with what they believe, it probably won't work. Will they stop loving each other for their differences? "Can two walk together, except they be agreed?" (Amos 3:3). Unless two people come together in agreement, there will be some kind of confusion. Can the believer stand the battle with the unbeliever's doubt in what he or she believes? The believer may ask questions like these: Am I going the wrong way again? Why am I so weak? Do I know that I am going the wrong way? Does my pastor at my church deal with these types of problems and if so how does he handle going the wrong way? Am I in the right relationship with this person? Why does everything I do keep failing? Why can't I keep a home? Why can't I keep a car? What is wrong with me?

Life will pass you by if you don't know where you are going in life. Have you ever traveled on the expressway or highway for a long period of time and finally come to your senses and realize that you might be going the wrong way? I remember picking up in a city called Brookhaven, Mississippi, one afternoon at the Walmart distribution center. I drove from midnight to my location and ended up in Nashville, Tennessee, when I was suppose to be in Nashville, Arkansas. I just drove the wrong way and never double-checked my paperwork to see if I was correct. I just kept driving. When I got there the next morning, I had to call my company and tell them that I had gone the wrong way. I lost money, and the company did too.

Sometimes when we are not paying attention to what we are doing, we can easily make a mistake like this. If you just continue to live in this world, you will have your experiences. Now you may say that you can't help but go down the wrong path because of how you were brought up. Our past does affect our future until we realize what keeps us from our destiny. Then it won't affect us anymore. There was a movie called *Wrong Turn*. Five friends were traveling together on vacation. They made it to a fork in the road, and they waited for a few seconds to decide which way they were going to go. They made their choice and went down a road that jeopardized all of their lives. Only two out of the five of them made it out to tell the story. You see, when we are not patient and make decisions without fully thinking a thing through, we always hurt ourselves.

Ask yourself these questions: Am I always rushing and then realize I have left something important at home that I really need? Am I an impatient person? Do I rush through cooking dinner?

We were born imperfect creatures in the flesh, but patience will keep us from making a wrong turn because, when we have time to think about our actions, we make the right decisions. When we are humble and obedient to the truth, the truth will keep us from a lot of pain. I have learned from the Lord that, when he gives me instructions, I must follow them because his instructions keep me from feeling the pain. No one likes pain, but sometimes we put ourselves in situations to feel the pain. Are you one of those people who are curious about everything? Are you the person who hangs out with people just to be cool even though you know that they are not on your level? Are you always taking advice from people who don't do what they say they are going to do? Are you tired of going the wrong way? Are you not ready to get your life together?

If you feel as if your world is upside down and you have no friends, and you feel as if you are just going through the motions, confess your problems to someone you believe in. Once you confess that you are tired of your situation, and you begin to make changes toward your situation, that's when the healing begins. You see, we can overcome anything when we ask our Lord and Savior Jesus Christ. He is the way, the truth, and the light. He is our strength when we need a lift. He is our protector in the midst of making a wrong turn. He is the one who leads and guides. When we trust our Lord and do what he tells us to do, his word is a lamp unto our feet, and a light unto our path (Psalm 119:105) we will not be led the wrong way.

Whether it be good, or whether it be evil,
we will obey the voice Lord our God, to
whom we send thee: that it may be well with
us, when we obey the voice of the Lord our
God. (Jeremiah 42:6)

Chapter 14

MY DESTINATION IS HEAVEN

Heaven is the place where I will spend eternal life. My understanding of my Bible is that the foundation of heaven is carved of precious stones. The streets are paved with gold. The walls are of shining pearl, and the breathtaking water of life flows through it. You have a choice to make for your life. Heaven is going to be home for my life. It was meant for man to rule and reign on this earth that we live on now, while the Lord would continue to rule and reign in the heavens above, but man chose to violate God's instructions, which left us in a place of sin. So, we must leave here to reunite with the Lord where there is no sin, and this will happen in heaven.

I feel as if I am in heaven already when my mind is at

peace. I feel joy because, even in the midst of trouble, I still feel at ease. I can't explain the feeling I get when I seek God. Everyone wants to choose heaven to be home, but some have already accepted that they can't get there because they can't be forgiven, but I believe we all can be forgiven through confession. Some people believe that life ends here on this earth as it does for animals, because they don't believe in a place called heaven above.

I believe that, if an individual doesn't choose to walk with God and follow his instructions, he or she will go to hell. Do I believe hell is real? I do. Just as I believe that heaven is real. You see, if people say they are going to live their lives the way they want and do anything they want without following the commandments that were given, then they have already chosen hell to be their destination.

I would like to encourage every person to understand that living in unforgiveness will keep you from God because, if you can't forgive your fellow neighbor when God has forgiven you, it is only fair for you to realize what is keeping you from being at peace with yourself and God.

When Jesus was on the cross, the people laughed and even spit on him. They were mocking him and saying, "If you are the Lord, why don't you get yourself down?" So, while the Lord hung on the cross, he said to God, "Father, forgive them; for they know not what they do" (Luke 23:34).

The Lord was the first to release unforgiveness. My heart goes out to every man and woman who feels he or she is going to heaven because he or she has done a lot of good deeds. But I am here to tell you that good deeds alone are not going to be enough because, without a relationship with the Lord, you will miss this peaceful destination. In the beginning, it was God who established the heavens and earth by word, and according to his word, a born-again believer of Jesus the Christ wins in the end, and Satan loses. You see, hell is a place where Satan rules and reigns. He is the chief demon of all demonic forces. He is the head musician in wicked music. He comes to steal, to kill, and destroy. You see, Satan rules hell, and he is busy trying to persuade as many souls as he can to follow after him, which is unrighteousness. This place called hell is hotter than lava. You will be cast into outer darkness, and there shall be weeping and gnashing of teeth (Matthew 8:12). The scripture advises that, once the devil deceives you, you will be cast into the lake of fire and brimstone where the beast and all the false prophets will be, and you will be tormented day and night for ever and ever. (Revelations 20:10). I don't want to imagine living my life to find out that this is where I am going to end up when I can live according to the Lord's instructions and know for sure where I am going.

Many have gone to hell because of disobedience, and

many went to hell and came back because God gave them an out-of-body experience so they would know that this place is real. I can assure you that, by following the road map in the Bible, which the Lord left for us over 2,000 years ago, and not the road map in the atlas, we will have a place prepared for us in heaven. You see, my eternal residence will be in heaven, but if someone wanted to contact or locate me here on this earth, they would need my physical address, which is another place I call heaven when I am away from what is going on in the world.

The choices we make through the rest of our lives will determine if we will keep our place in the kingdom called heaven. Do you know where you are going when you die? Are you living your life to only reap earthly things, or are you living to reap heavenly things? The Lord's word says, "Lay not up for yourselves treasures upon earth, where moth and rust doth corrupt, and where thieves break through and steal: But lay up for yourselves treasures in heaven, where neither moth nor rust doth corrupt, and where thieves do not break through nor steal" (Matthew 6:19–20).

I understand that I can't live an ungodly life if I want to see heaven. I can't imagine going to hell. I know the God I serve sees everything I do, so I must sow to him and not to the world. I have learned that, if I sow more to my flesh, my flesh will reap corruption, but if I sow more to my spirit, it

The Life of a Praying Owner-Operator

will reap everlasting life (Galatians 6:7–8). I choose to be heaven bound. I want to live where there's no more pain, no more sickness or diseases, no more deaths, and no more sad days. The alternative is a trip to hell where there is a lake of fire, gnashing of teeth, and the experience of being tormented over and over for the rest of my life. What do you choose?

My sisters and brothers, to learn if you have a place in the kingdom called heaven, I would like you to turn in the Bible to the gospel of John 3:16 and to Revelation 21:6–8. These verses will let you know if you have a place in the kingdom. But if you haven't accepted the Lord as Lord over your life, the time is now. Perhaps you were in fellowship with God, but have been so busy with work that you have lost this fellowship. If you have never connected, or if you are ready to reconnect please pray this prayer with me:

> Heavenly Father, I acknowledge that I am a sinner. I repent for all my sins against you. Lord, forsake all that I have done. I ask that you come into my life and save me, and I believe by the confession from my mouth and the commitment from my heart that you died and rose for me. Lord, I receive your salvation, and by faith I am saved in Jesus's name. Lord

I thank you daily for the spiritual roadmap that you left to lead and guide me, which is the Holy Spirit. I thank you, Lord, for the physical road map that directs me down the right road daily, which is the Holy Bible, and I tell you that I am so grateful and thankful for a place you created called Heaven.

This is the bread which cometh down from heaven, that a man eat thereof, and not die. I am the living bread which cometh down from heaven: If any man eat of this bread, he shall live forever: and the bread that I will give is my flesh, which I give for the life of the world. (John 6:50–51)

NOTES

Chapter 1: The Life of Trucking

What is your purpose for sitting behind the wheel of a tractor-trailer or other vehicle?

Chapter 2: Traveling Is a Blessing

When you make it from point A to point B with no distraction, how do you feel?

Chapter 3: Getting Up Early and Lying Down Late

How can getting up early be profitable in your life?

Chapter 4: Praying All Around the Clock

Why do we usually pray only when there is trouble, and don't understand that we must pray when there is happiness also?

Chapter 5: Can't Make It Home for Dinner

How do you feel when you miss an important dinner or gathering?

Chapter 6: My Destination Is Coming Up

What kind of relief do you get when you make it to where you are going safely?

Chapter 7: Honey, I'm Home

What kind of smile do you get when you walk into your home? Are you excited about being loved?

Chapter 8: No Stress: All the Bills Are Paid

How does it feel to have all your bills paid and still have money left over?

Chapter 9: Never Get Out of Your Truck

We should never be in a rush to get out of our vehicle in the dark when no one else is around when we think, but do not know for sure, that we see an accident.

Chapter 10: Treat Every Trip Like a Vacation

When was the last time you went on a vacation and enjoyed yourself away from work?

Chapter 11: Breaker One Nine

"What's your twenty?" means where are you? Have you figured out why you are here and where you are going in this life?

Chapter 12: Trucking Is a Career

Does your job make you necessary in this world? Do you have a license for this job? Can you move anywhere in the country with this license? This is a career.

Chapter 13: Going the Wrong Way

Have you ever been traveling for a while and noticed you were going the wrong way? Are you living to accomplish the things of the world or things of heaven?

Chapter 14: My Destination Is Heaven

Do you know for sure where you are going when you die?

BIBLE GUIDE

A Psalm of David: The Twenty-Third Psalm:

The Lord is my shepherd; I shall not want.
He maketh me to lie down in green pastures:
he leadeth me beside the still waters.
He restoreth my soul: he leadeth me in the
paths of righteousness for his name's sake.
Yea, though I walk through the valley of
the shadow of death, I will fear no evil: for
thou art with me; thy rod and thy staff they
comfort me.
Thou preparest a table before me in the
presence of mine enemies: thou anointest my
head with oil; my cup runneth over.
Surely goodness and mercy shall follow me
all the days of my life: and I will dwell in the
house of the Lord forever.

TRUCKER GUIDE

 Psalm of Milam

The Lord is my truck; He is my Transport;
He is my provider.

He maketh me lie down in my truck and rest;
He leadeth me on the expressway in peace.

My mind is clear, and my thoughts are free;
He restoreth my soul when he rescued me.

Yea, though I drive through the wilderness
of the shadow of death, I will fear no evil: for
thou art my protection: thy shield and thy
power they comfort me.

When thou feed me, He feed me with fruits
of righteousness: fruits of joy, peace, and long
suffering; thou anointed me in the presence
of my enemies.

Surely grace and mercy shall follow me all the
days of my life: and I will dwell in the house
of the Lord forever.